Scribes Press. http://www.ScribesPress.com

Printed in the United States of America
First Printing: June 2014

ISBN: 978-0-9937615-4-6

Community Planning

&

Introduction

Implementation

Introduction

Community Planning and Implementation is a guide and outline to a new initiative that is being implemented on a global basis. The implementation will be rolled out over the next few years, and will include more interactive ways of doing things, giving feedback, and ofcourse implementing those actions.

- **The Royal Queen Support Services System**

A universal help grid designed to respond to the needs of the individual and the community. Where you need it, when you need. Described as being one of the most efficient support service system ever created.

- **The Royal Threat Assessment Team Office**

New ways of efficiently and effectively finding solutions to situations that might be ongoing within individuals situations, communities, and environments. .

- **The Royal Order**

A Universal Force for a universal objective. They are likely to play a pivotal role in future
endeavors.

- **The Royal Queen Security Clearances**

A new way of keeping communities and the individual safer, as they go about their daily lives. These work in conjunction with the unique identifier system.

- **The Royal Queen Standards Bureau**

This offices aligns spiritual objectives and standards, and ensures that there is an alignment, a harmonized standards of operating, and operations.

- **The Maximum and Minimum Holding Facilities**

An alignment of standards designed to assist communities with finding solutions to situations of a penal nature that are happening within communities.

- **Education**

The Royal Queen standards of Learning. Giving future generations access to education that makes sense. Greater access, and implementation.

- **Health Care**

Access to low cost, effective health care. Access to health care that makes sense. Fast, safe, efficient and efficient.

- **Databases**

Accurate and helpful databases. Information is easily updated, and they are accurate and inline with the new standards.

- **Social Psychologists**

Social Psychologists will be taking on a greater role in community implementation and planning.   The future is

- **Community Advisors**

Well educated, well versed individuals that are interested in playing a role within the community.

- **Bill 184**

The chance to become the correct person, the chance to do the correct thing.

The future has real potential for change that makes sense, and that works.

Community Planning

&

Table

Of

Contents

Implementation

Table Of Contents

Community Planning

&

Community Planning

&

Implementation

Implementation

Community Implementation and Planning

A Global Plan, for a global initiative. The idea is to have a harmonized plan of implementation that can benefit most individuals across the face of the planet. It means connecting with various sources on a global basis to implement plans of action, and activities that enable humanity to be thee eligible to be in the correct situations, and it's in line with all the objectives.

The idea is to have a holistic approach to communities. I prefer to not have homogenized communities, but I do want to have communities where you can walk in, and have a familiar look and feel.

There should be some basics that makes sense to everyone, or just about everyone. The basics that are likely to make the most sense are things such as:

The Royal Queen Security Clearances
The HELP ME GRID
Unique Identifiers

A universal cash exchange system similar to The Royal Queen Authority Financial System may also make sense, it would be nice to see, but not necessarily essential. Basic community changes, and items are what will be implemented across the board.

The Royal Threat Assessment Team Office

The Office, handles situations and finds solutions. The office is there to be ever present, not ever visulent. They actually deal with the individuals that are problematic for the society, vs creating files on individuals that do not need to be tracked and monitored. They are updated spiritually on a regular and on going basis. The link in with several different sources, to create one of the most effective situation, solutions on the face of the planet.

The Royal Queen Support Services System

The HELP ME GRID is a universal help me grid system. It files reports on behalf of individuals. It's there to assist, and it links in and connects with several other such systems.

The system has been planned, and is an essential part of community planning and implementation. It's there to assist communities and individuals in their day to day lives. The system takes, and files spiritual based reports, which are then now aligned synchronized, and harmonized with current systems.

Filing a spiritual report, it then links in with other systems, it then links in with earth based, and universal systems, or components. Those reports are then actioned.

The Royal Order

A Universal Force for a universal objective. The Royal Order is likely to play a pivitol role in future endeavors. They are a league designed to assist with a variety of situations, and they find solutions that are universal and unique. They are well trained in some cases, or activated on an ongoing and rotational basis. They are eligible to assist with the correct situation. We believe that when the correct person is called into the correct situation, at the correct moment and time, it can create monumental changes and effects in a ways that benefits the society as a whole.

They are alert hopefully, ever more increasingly active, they have the spiritual authority over ever other force, and hopefully in future will play an increasingly more pivitol role in community planning and implementation.

The Royal Queen Standards Bureau

This offices aligns spiritual objectives and standards, and ensures that there is an alignment, a harmonized standards of operating, and operations

The Maximum and Minimum Holding Facilities
The Royal Queen Institutions of Learning (Education)
Health Care

The Maximum and Minimum Holding Facilities

The Maximum and minimum holding facilities play a substantial role in community planning and implementation, and what will be occurring every more increasingly is that when a crime is commuted, and penal intervention is required, the holding facilities will pay a unique role, possibly along with The Office, in evaluating those individuals, and ensuring that penal time spiritually is in universal alignment.

This means if a situation does occur, a crime is committed, or something where penal intervention is required, both objectives, and time that is required, will now be harmonized.

Filing a spiritual report, and having it linking in with the earth province component, and then, having those reports being actioned.

Databases

The databases in most cases have been aligned and are more in line with objectives. With the current databases information didn't always have the accuracy that was required. With these new databases that use and utilize the Unique Identifier system, information is more correct and accurate.

The databases can also have more concise and correct information. Who was in the incident, relevant and suitable details can be included, while still respecting the privacy of the individual. In an emergency information can be also tracked more accurately and responded to in an more effective mannerism.

Social Psychologists

Social Psychologists play a huge role in community implementation and planning. They have the harmonized skill set that is necessary to get the situations aligned and in order. Their unique view of situations play a pivitol and universal role in community implementation and planning.

They have a duo skill set that focuses on the social, but also the psychological aspects of the situations. Previous situation focused on the psychology of the situation, and at times neglected, negated, or flat out ignored the social, or underlying social aspects. These are all now taken into consideration with this newly implemented format of doing things.

Community Advisors

These are individuals in their own capacities that care about their communities, and have a beneficial effect upon the community. They are aware of the situations that are ongoing and take measures to implement, or enact changes that assist, have a positive changes or affect the community in a beneficial manner.

They are consistent and they make sense. Some will or will not have the social psychologist, possibly researcher, background, but they will be or will have played a positive role in their communities.

Bill 184

The chance to become the correct person, the chance to do the correct thing. One of the most comprehensive Bills ever written. Written by The Royal Queen, Royal Queen Georgia Marie Bailey. The law would enable a generation to be eligible to be protected and kept safe.

Education

Standards that are in line, on par, or in semi alignment with The Royal Queen Institutions of Learning, and access to education or information.

Each student should have the chance to become the correct person, doing the correct thing, and they should have the chance and opportunity for a reasonable amount of time.

Health Care

I would like to implemented a system of health care and reforms that benefit that vast majority of individuals. I would like to see that health care distributed for free, or at a reasonable cost to the individual. The mechanisms are there in place, and individuals should be given access to information.

I would like to see Personal Identifiers used as a source of evaluations, comprehensive evaluations that seriously make sense. Once the evaluations are done, I would like to then see methods implemented for treatment, therapy, or both for a reasonable cost.

I would like to see the heath care system link in with alternative systems thus a holistic application to treatment could be implemented. If community Councillors are needed, medical professional, social psychologists, remote Councillors, financial well being assistance, and so forth, that could be instituted.

Functionality and Flow

The system that is being created, or that has been created is one of flow and functionality. Hopefully a system or situation that seriously makes sense. It is harmonized with spiritual based, earth province, and universal systems.

The system must be versatile and it must function. I would like to see the vast majority of previous dsyfunctionality discontinue.
versatile, and it must function.

The current systems, cost lives, money, the vast majority of individuals operating are operating over their budgets, because the current system does not have the financial functionality it needs to survive. It also cost innocent people their lives, I can cocognizant this, by the string of innocent individuals that have been affected by these current systems.

The individuals in these situations are starting to use spiritual based situations to record, file reports, do investigations, and that is the reason mini conspiracies are literally also being recorded. It's a fresh start in the way things are done.

Changes need to be made, they need to be implemented and planned. Those changes however need to be made by those who are not too dsyfunctional, they need to be made by those who are functional enough to comprehend that a change needs to be made.

Some positions are likely better off, if they are not infiltrated situations such as the informant system. Some who were on this system, have remained unchanged, and thus could be still eligible to play a vital role in creating situations, and giving helpful suggestion, feedback and advise to specific parts of community planning and implementation. We are always, or often willing to work with functional individuals.

There are some hard and fast rules, some versatile rules, but primarily, those waste of space and time and energies that are a continual pattern of misbehavior, bad deeds, deliberately socially disruptive, criminally inclined, need to be curtailed, and either placed into better streams, of social action, or thought, or they need to be curtailed in a way that makes sense to the society, and if possible to the individual.

Phase II

A brief introduction to the next phase in Community Planning and Implementation. It shows you how the paying their annual fees and entries fees can now be used and utilized to provide entire communities with a comprehensive evaluation that will enable communities to become aware of the needs within the community, problems if they are occurring, and possible solutions that could be implemented, or utilized.

Phase II is an ongoing comprehensive look at communities, the individuals, and the community as a whole. It shows you how communities can achieve additional funding. Ways to save money, cut down on time wasted, and become more efficient.

Communities once evaluated can then look at individual situations within the community, but then situations at a whole. They can implement solutions in minutes, rather than hours or days. A faster more efficient structure. That will hopefully make sense.

Community Planning

&

Reporting

Forms

Implementation

Reporting Forms

Reporting Forms For Social Behaviours

The form is sent in when other interactions or feedback has failed. They are given a chance to correct behaviour before an actual threat assessment file is created, penal or other more direct and overt action has to be taken.

Step 1

The person is first given a verbal feedback or warning. Usually via an email

Step 2

The Form takes the initial report if the situation continues. The form also gives vital and crucial feedback.

Step 3

Corrective action is initiated. If the behavior continues, additional action is taken

Step 4

The Form links in with other departments and divisions.

Eg. If penal action is required, it will link in with the Maximum or Minimum holding facilities.

The Office is another location the form could link in with

The Form could also link in with the call center but that is less likely

The Form coul link in with the Standards Bureau

The Form could even link in with Investigations

The Form could link in with Social Psychologists and or Community Advisors

The Form could even link in with Community Planning and Implementation

The Form could link in with Legal Division

The Form could link in with Remote Councillor

The Form can and likely does work in conjunction with The Royal Queen Support Services System.

Step 5

Additional Action is taken and documented. If the behaviour continues.

Step 6
The Form continues to document and take the additional action that is needed, until the situation is resolved in a satisfactory manner.

They can be made billable. If their anti or unsuitable social behaviour, or behaviors are costing the society quite a bit as a whole or at large, and thus the result. They are participating in unsuitable or lowest common denominator social behaviour.

Reporting Forms Customer Service

The form works with the Unique Identifier System. It records confirms the individual that is calling in, and it keeps track of the situation, and stays or remains open, until a solution is found.

Step 1

The Form is opened when a customer calls in. In some cases. The form is filled out with the person and the nature of the call.

Step 2

The reason that it could not be initially resolved, and any further or additional action that is needed for the situation to be resolved.

Step 3

Once the correct action has been taken, then the form can be closed.

Reporting Forms Standards Bureau

The form is opened when there is a conflict of interest, or an irregularity with the standards that are required.

The form works within literally all aspect of society within A New Kingdom. Eg.

The Service Industry
Health Care
Education
Government
Military
Customer Service
Online and Offline Services

Step 1

A form is opened when there is an incident or an irregularity with the standards.

Step 2

A helpful suggestion is made at that point if the situation can be resolved, or deescalated by making the helpful suggestion, or giving, vital, suitable, and relevant feedback.

Step 3

If that is not possible, then the form links in with various other locations, offices, or services. Literally just about every aspect of society. Eg.

Local Police

If penal action is required, it will link in with the Maximum or Minimum holding facilities.

The Office is another location the form could link in with

The Form could also link in with the call center

The Form coul link in with the Standards Bureau

The Form could even link in with Investigations

The Form could link in with Social Psychologists and or Community Advisors

The Form could even link in with Community Planning and Implementation

The Form could link in with Legal Division

Social Services

Government Offices

Military

Step 4

Corrective action is taken, and the form continues to be documented, and the various departments are linked in with until the matter is resolved or the issue is properly escalated, and then it can be shown why there either was, or was not a resolution.

Investigation Forms

This form is opened and used for Royal Queen Investigations. (An office belonging to The Royal Queen) The form is opened at the start of Investigations, and remains opened until the situation is resolved to a suitable conclusion, or if it could not be for some reason, then will also document that as well, in advance.

The form also uses the Unique Identifier System, to confirm the identity of the clients, and those involved in the situation.

A live update of the form could be sent to the client during the course of the investigation, or if that is not eligible, a copy of the form could be sent to the client at the conclusion of the investigation. If not in most cases, a summarized copy of the form will be sent out to the client, enabling them to see some of the steps taken, and or just the outcome of the investigation.

The form is Uniquely Identified, and thus only the correct individual, with the specific access that is eligible may review the form.

Community Planning

&

Social

Coordinators

Implementation

Social Coordinators

The Social Worker System is one that touches many aspect of various lives. Social Workers are at times in contact with employers, parole officers, schools, councils, police, other emergency workers, and a variety of other individuals. They are working and coordinating on a daily basis. Often they may or may not have adequate support, or funding to achieve the objectives that they wish to. Some are underpaid, and over worked.

In revamping the social worker system, we first took a look at Community Planning and Implementation, and the goals, objectives, and requirements, for the ideas that are in place. The goal was to find a suitable and effective way to revamp much of the system. Find cost effective ways to cut down on some of the procedures in place. Reporting procedures could also be streamlined and utilized, to save time, money, and to be more efficient.

The Social Worker System is just one of many systems that are being reviewed and revamped. It's one system that we will take a closer look at, but it's one of many within a new structure, that will hopefully be appealing and will make sense to the vast majority of individuals.

Funding for these systems will also be more accessible, and will be applied and applicable where the system really makes sense.

Revamping A System Of Abuse

The social worker system had become not as effective as first hoped or thought, so a new scheme or mechanism could be added to enable it to become more effective. To that means to that end.

Social Workers from here on in to be referenced as Social Coordinators.

1. They are to have limited to no contact with the informant system. While working this cuts down on influence that might be adverse to the jobs that they are fulfilling. They are required to leave this system, and influence outside of their place of employment, and their community, social coordination decisions.

2. Social Coordinators need to have adequate pay, housing, re-sources, sleep, support. To achieve this objective, the system needed to be revamped in a way to cut cost, save time, and supply a support network that suitably and adequately made sense. The support network would be readily available to those in the correct situations, doing the correct things.

3. Social Coordinators should be paid and funded for their time and energy, so that those actually putting in the time and energy have adequate pay and support. To that end, effort should equal adequate pay, support and funding. Funding and the way it's implemented could be revamped.

4. Social Coordinators should be properly and adequately protected, and kept safe. In the course of doing their job, or their duty to the community and others, they at times are set upon in unfortunate, and unsuitable ways, that do not make sense.

5. Socially they also need to be supported. Linking in with Social/Psychologist, Community Advisors, and others would likely make a difference, and enable them to have better or more adequate support. Use of remote councillors as a tool might also be effective and helpful. The social support network, should have the capacity to review and make recommendations, anonymously.

6. Child Abusers are requested and required to sign a spiritual document, a spiritual form that confirms their desire to discontinue with any ongoing abuse, and another form that does or does not track such ongoing abuses. The document is listed as a reverse form, and it's to assist with preventing abuse.

7. The Royal Threat Assessment Team Office can if necessary be utilized to create Threat Assessment Team File is that becomes a necessary part of their function. Files can be created and actioned on a regular and ongoing basis, if necessary.

8. Spiritual Based Products and Services could be supplied to enable social coordinators. To that means and that end, The Royal Queen will be making a significant contribution to enable the situation to commence.

- Access to If this song should be sung records
- If this accident could be prevented
- If this crime should be prevented
- If this crime should be committed
- Remote Personal Assistant Service
- Remote Councillors
- HELP ME GRID
- Guardian Protect Me Service

9. Care, Maintenance and Governance should work in conjunction to the services already being provided, to assist Social Coordinators with their efforts.

10. Social Coordinators can also in future link in with The Royal Order, a spiritual based fleet, that are designed to assist with a variety of situations.

11. Also when children are in care, they need to be located in places of care that make sense.

12. Social Coordinators could link in also with The Blue Amber alert system, a system designed and created by The Royal Queen, Royal Queen Georgia Marie Bailey. It provides an alert when a child goes missing, or is taken without permission.

13. Proper efficient, and continual use of the Social Behavior Reporting Forms. These forms and documents were again created by The Royal Queen, to enable communities, and society as a whole, to better keep track of situations, until solutions were found.

14. Limit unnecessary involvement of police, parole officers, and anyone who may or may not assist with the intended goals, objectives, or of the social coordinators.

15. Frequency Suits could be provided to Social Coordinators to assist them with their ongoing efforts to follow up with clients, and the children that they are responsible for, who are in their care. Eg. If there is an alert. The frequency suits would have to record all their visits and keep a track of their activities, as long as the agreement, and arrangements are in place in advance.

16. Bill 184 when applicable or eligible should be a part of the procedures and part of the ongoing system utilized. Also any additional Rules and Regulations belonging to The Royal Queen, that might be appropriate or eligible.

17. The Unique Identifier System could also be used to assist with anonymously identifying children and keeping them safe. It can also be used to enable Social Coordinators. They can have a degree of anonymity when filing reports.

18. Create a circle of trust, and responsibility of who social workers can and do report to. They need to be clear that their feedback will be adequately actioned, and that they will have the support that they need.

19. They could also be provided with monthly discounts on their housing or rental units. These are discounts based on an ongoing evaluation. A outcome of a job well done. Part of the bonuses for a job actually well done.

It's an active future where hopefully the citizens take a more active and open part in their communities. It means that we have people in positions and situations of trust. It's a future that is sustainable, by looking at a more holistic approach to communities, and how they function.

It's a future where people are actually and actively rewarded for the work that they do, for the time and the energy that they put into activities, or just serving the community. It's a plan of action and interaction that makes sense.

Community Planning and Implementation creates safe communities, faster ways of reporting and actioning ideas. It enables citizens to take a more active role, it's modern, efficient, and it makes sense.

Community Planning

&

Phase II

Implementation

Phase II

Paying The Annual Fee and Entry Fee

Community Planning and Implementation takes on an additional direction. You can now remotely implement Phase II for communities. The initiative provides more options and opportunities.

The person with the correct authority within the community, can now request that the entire community receive a comprehensive evaluation. The evaluation begins by remotely, requesting your community pay their annual fee and entry fee. If it is not the decision maker making the request at the moment, the request will put you in touch with the decision maker for that specific, or peculiar feature. The local community member that can initiate the feature, can. The request begins a comprehensive evaluation that is done on behalf of the community, and the individuals in that community. The request is usually initiated by decision makers for the community. Local politicians, community leaders, elected representatives, or others.

The request begins a comprehensive evaluation of your community, the individuals in the community and the resources. It enables the individuals, communities and those in positions of responsibility to be eligible.

The comprehensive analysis enables the community to be evaluated for several core factors that are important and essential to every community. They are evaluated socially, financially, economically, etc. Any social or community situations that could be problematic, or potentially problematic are evaluated. What is also evaluated are the needs of the community, the individuals in those communities, and resources that are available.

The comprehensive evaluation, evaluates risks to the community, if any member needs to serve punitive time, which resources, known and unknown are eligible to the individual and the community as a whole. Eg. There are several initiatives that might be available to a community such as funding for special initiatives, or to the individual such as remote councilor, free medical information, etc.

The whole process is very quick and easy, also it enables you to be cognizant if your community is eligible for additional funding or resources under The Royal Queen's, community planning and implementation initiative. The whole community is also linked in, to other resources, that might be eligible for them as a whole or individually.

Community Pays it's annual fee and entry fee

Requesting that the community that you are a part of pay it's annual fee and entry fee get's the ball rolling on community planning and implementation phase two. This provides the entire community with a comprehensive evaluation, and enables funding that the community may not previously have had access to before.

Community Evaluation

The community as a whole is evaluated. They are evaluated to see if there are any ongoing problems or issues in the community. They evaluate collectively, and individually. They also evaluate if there are any ongoing issue that need to be taken care of.

The community evaluation is highly comprehensive. Similar community evaluations could take years, months, or even weeks, and cost millions upon millions of dollars. We enable community evaluation in a matter of minutes, and give you the results when you need them. That way you can begin fixing, repairing, or reevaluating the things that need to be done for your community.

Funding

Funding is then doled out to the community based on this ongoing evaluation. If a community is taking care of it's needs, responsibilities, it's entitled to the funding that it is deserving of. Too often efforts of some communities are over looked in favor of other situation. This is a more fair, and equitable evaluation process.

Funding is doled out in two parts. There is a spiritual based funding portion to the evaluation. That is doled out first. Then funding for the community is also evaluated and doled out as well. Funding is either released right away in full depending on the community, and or released on a daily, weekly, monthly, quarterly, semi-annual, or annual basis. This way communities can make decisions, and see which items around a community need to be given priority.

Linked In

Community Planning and implementation links in with every aspect of the community. They do a spiritually comprehensive evaluation of the community and the individuals in the community. Community Planning and implementation then links in with the services already in the community. If they in line with the community and planning implementation requirements, they can be given the details required to bring the service up to par, with community planning and implementation.

They link in with community services, local situations that make sense, and any other service, or situation that is suitable or eligible for that community and standards that are in line with community planning and implementation.

They link in with the penal system, schools, hospitals, health care services, mental health care services, councillors, social psychologists, community advisors, social/community councilors, (formerly social workers), spiritual based services, The Office (Royal Threat Assessment Team Office), Maximum and minimum holding facilities.

Rating System

There is a new rating system under community planning and implementation. It rates the efficiency to which each community is responsible. Do they do repairs, answer calls, are they prompt, efficient. Do they use cost saving measures when possible? Are they a good neighbor? All these and many more questions are factored in to give each community a correct and accurate rating. Spiritual ratings are also factored into the rating system now, so that you have a comprehensive idea of what is ongoing.

Community Alert

There are two kinds of community alerts. Mandatory community alerts, and additional alerts that one can subscribe to.

Under the new system, places, locations, and other receive an alert if there is an incident, or if there is an individual, or a situation that is ongoing. The alert give the individual, or community a cursory view of what is on-going, and enables you to make better comprehensive and concise decisions about the individuals using your services, or even entering your location, or premises.

The second portion to the community alert is a detailed service one can pay for, it provides a comprehensive view of what is ongoing. It provides additional details, and information about incidents, thus you can have a more comprehensive view if you are the type of person that is eligible to have that type of access.

Reasons and Responsibilities

Under community planning and implementation, each community is now responsible for a neighboring community, and they take care of the problems ongoing in that city. If the city has a broken item they attempt to fix it or replace it. They cover the cost for that community. If the community is wasteful, then it needs to find better way of doing things, and if there is an ongoing situation, they find ways to assist with mitigating and managing.

Most city repair or replace their own damage, and in most cases that does works great, but if there is an ongoing problem, sometimes it can be hidden, or fall through the cracks. This way with neighboring cities actively involved, it's in everyone's interest to fix, repair, replace, the damage in an equitable time frame.

Eg. The city of South Hampton for example, now would take care of Walkers Hamlet. The smaller location has several million dollars worth of damage that needs to be repaired or replaced. The items are fixed the problems are solved in a suitable manner. Thus South Hampton has a suitable rating, and has assisted with the problem, thus likely also suitable funding.

The problem is not repaired or the damage keeps reoccurring. If the damage keeps reoccurring, then we know that there is a problem, or a potential problem in Walker's Hamlet and the problem needs to be resolved as soon as possible. This would not work well towards the rating of South Hampton, because they are failing to fix the problem, that they are responsible for.

The problem is fixed, but keeps occurring. Thus South Hampton is cognizant that there is a potential problem in Walker's Hamlet that needs to be taken care of. They can then use comprehensive measures to see what the problem is, and how best to go about mitigating and managing it.

The city that you are responsible for, can also assist with determining your funding. If eg. South Hampton does a good job of taking care of Walker's Hamlet, and the hamlet is in good condition, then funding is also in part based on this. The problems are looked into and assisted with.

The odd time, a major world city may participate, in assisting with community planning and implementation for an adjoining or loosely affiliated world city, town, hamlet. Most times however it is local cities assisting local cities, enabling community planning and implementation to make sense.

The odd time if there is not a neighboring city near by, a city may be asked to be enabled for it's own situations for a time, until a new city, or neighbouring bureau can be enabled.

How problems are handled

Community Planning and Implementation is similar to other initiatives, and yet slightly different. Eg. It's not that we are not cognizant of the broken window theory, but we do things slightly differently. If there is a problem in one area, it could be a source of problems in other areas, that much is true, and problems need to be, and should be handled in a prompt, and equanimicable fashion that does suitably make sense.

If a individual is problematic in one area, that individual is just as likely to be problematic in other areas.

Community Planning

&

Future

Implementation

Future

Community Planning and Implementation and what it means. It hopefully means a brighter happier more efficient future. A future where ideas are implemented in a reasonable frame of time. Where we have the correct ideas implemented in days, or weeks, or months vs years.

It's an active future where hopefully the citizens take a more active and open part in their communities. It means that we have people in positions and situations of trust. It's a future that is sustainable, by looking at a more holistic approach to communities, and how they function.

It's a future where people are actually and actively rewarded for the work that they do, for the time and the energy that they put into activities, or just serving the community. It's a plan of action and interaction that makes sense.

Community Planning and Implementation creates safe communities, faster ways of reporting and actioning ideas. It enables citizens to take a more active role, it's modern, efficient, and it makes sense.

www.ingramcontent.com/pod-product-compliance
Lightning Source LLC
Chambersburg PA
CBHW071759020426
42331CB00008B/2331